Making the most of CHRISTMAS

Contents

IDEAS FOR FAMILY SERVICE TALKS

➤ ➤ ➤ ➤ ➤ ➤ *GIVING*

John 3:16

| Visual aids: | *Huge, brightly-coloured stocking in the shape of a 'J' pulled up high into the chancel arch* |

Ask about presents. Has anyone received something special?

Pull the stocking up into the roof (if it is not already in place). Talk about the joy of receiving exactly what you wanted and the disappointments if you don't.

Talk about children and adults who have nothing given to them, or who have gifts but not the thing they want most – the love of parent(s).

Christmas is about God's giving. It is an expression of his love.

Refer to the stocking. The letter 'J' refers to someone very special – Jesus. Explain that he is God's gift.

Conclusion: It is good to receive, but also good to give. Jesus said, 'It is more blessed to give than to receive' (Acts 20:35). Giving is of the nature of God even though we don't deserve it. If his nature is in us we will be glad to give and receive.

➤ ➤ ➤ ➤ ➤ ➤ *THE GIFT*

2 Corinthians 9:15

| Visual aids: | *Large, colourfully-wrapped box* |

Talk about presents.

A child walks in with a large box. It is addressed to you, from the person who loves you most of all! You ponder aloud what its contents might be.

You decide not to open it, giving your reasons. Explore possible loss, disappointment of giver, etc. and apply this to God's gift of Jesus.

Then change your mind! What could it be? Label says it is the most important thing in the world to know: how to come into a living relationship with God. Explain why that is important. We are either friends or enemies of God, now and for ever.

Conclusion: Remind people of the importance of receiving from God what cannot be obtained by themselves.

'PEACE' OF CHRISTMAS CAKE

Luke 9:8-20

Visual aids:	Large cardboard cake in five slices, each slice with a letter clearly painted on the side

Show cake. Show the five slices as being part of the whole (without showing the letters). Make the point that there are many things we do over Christmas, but it is really about one main thing. The five slices remind us in five ways of that main meaning.

Explore the Bible reading by teaching that Christmas is:

❏ verse 8: about the Poor (show first slice with P on it). Talk about the involvement of shepherds, probably both poor and socially despised. God is still concerned for the poor.

❏ verse 10: for Everyone (show second slice with E on it). Christmas still is for everyone.

❏ verses 10-11: something to be Announced (show third slice). It still is.

❏ verse 12: about a Child (show fourth slice). It still is.

Luke 1:31 and Matthew 1:23 are about God being with us or Emmanuel.

Hold up all the five slices with the letters clearly showing. Check that the words are remembered. Emphasize that Christmas and the life and work of Jesus is about these things.

Conclusion: May the P...E...A...C...E of Christmas be with you.

CRADLE, CROSS AND CROWN

Matthew 1:18-25

Visual aids:	A 2m cracker, containing a cradle, cross and crown, and with a large label saying, 'Something to tell you about Christmas'.

Investigate the huge cracker which is either brought in or has been on view all through the service.

Break it open. Take out the *cradle*. Tell the Christmas story. (But the response is, 'We know that!')

Lead in to the second object. Hold up the *cross*. Explain how Jesus could be 'Saviour', i.e. by showing us what God is like, what he requires of us and how he suffered and died to do away with the consequences of our wrong.

Lead in to the last object. Show the *crown*. Christ was, and is, someone special. He was and is God. He is like a king, and one day all will submit to him.

Conclusion: The cradle, cross and crown teach us about Christmas. No wonder it's such a joyful time.

CHRISTMAS LETTERS

Luke 2:1-20

Visual aids:	*A number of large envelopes containing short letters*

Imagine a competition with a large prize for letters which explain the meaning of Christmas. What sort of things might they say?

Open letters (about partly-wrong views):
- ❑ about no school, from Mr Muckabout
- ❑ about getting presents, from Master Grabbalot-and-never-say-thank-you
- ❑ about eating, from Mrs Scoffalot
- ❑ about drinking, from Lord Boozalot
  (Children can indicate whether they think the letters are right or wrong. Shout a loud 'No' at the end to make the point.)

Further letters (about truth):
- ❑ God with us, from Isaiah
- ❑ Saviour, from the angel Gabriel

Further letters (about response):
- ❑ No room, from the innkeeper
- ❑ Worship (gifts), from the wise men

Conclusion: What would *our* letter say? It might say something like: Christmas is about the birth of Jesus. He came into our world because we needed to know about God and how to be friends with him. And one day when we die we can be sure we are going to be with him for ever.

➤ ➤ ➤ ➤ ➤ ➤ # *JOURNEY TO BETHLEHEM*

Luke 2:3-5

Visual aids (optional):	*Large stable constructed somewhere in the church*

Parents and children go on a piggy-back ride through the church, ending with a discussion about how comfortable it was, and did they have a good donkey? etc. Then read this simple monologue which brings out the realities of the journey.

'It was 140 miles that journey from Nazareth to Bethlehem.

Seven whole days it took us, travelling through the daylight hours.

On the first day, the sun shone like gold in the sky – and we hoped and prayed for a warm place to stay.

On the second day, the wind blew like the one that parted the Red Sea for Moses – and we hoped and prayed for a warm place to stay.

On the third day, the rain came down like Noah's flood – and we hoped and prayed for a warm place to stay.

On the fourth day, the air was cold like ice – and we hoped and prayed for a warm place to stay.

On the fifth day, our hands were numb and our hearts heavy – and we hoped and prayed for a warm place to stay.

On the sixth day, the rains returned – and we hoped and prayed for a warm place to stay.

On the seventh day, we arrived at Bethlehem – and we hoped and prayed for a warm place to stay.

But there was no room at the inn.'

Conclusion: The end can be a good point to place the Advent candle in the window of the stable. The children can wake up the innkeeper with all sorts of whistles and rattles. This ties in well with the 'be vigilant' themes of Advent.

➤ ➤ ➤ ➤ ➤ ➤ # *PARCELS*

1 Corinthians 9:15

Visual aids:	*Wrapped parcels*

Children's minds are full of parcels and presents on Christmas morning. Using the idea of Christmas parcels will always hold their attention.

❑ You could have two parcels to show them, one glitzy and the other rather dull and badly wrapped. They could represent two types of Christmas. Inside the glitz wrapping might be an empty box; inside the other parcel a spare baby-Jesus crib figure.

❏ Two boxes could represent our gift to God (a picture of oneself) and God's gift to us (a crib figure).

❏ A large parcel, beautifully wrapped, could be delivered to the front of the church. (A 'postman' riding a push bike down the aisles is effective!) You can admire the beautiful packing, but fail to see the point in opening the present.

Conclusion: At Christmas we can focus on the trappings and miss the real gift.

BIRTHDAY CAKE

John 1:4-5

Visual aids:	*Birthday cake with magic candles*

Produce a birthday cake complete with candles and maybe with 'Happy Birthday Jesus' iced on it. Less inhibited children and congregations may like to sing 'Happy Birthday to you'. Light the candles and invite the children to blow them out. Use the 'magic candles' which always relight after being blown out (readily available from shops selling cake decorations).

Conclusion: After several children have tried to blow out the candles without success, refer to the light that shines in the darkness which will never go out.

IT'S NOT WORTH IT

Galatians 4:4-7

Visual aids:	*Christmas stocking, wrapped empty box, tele-messages*

Hang a stocking in the pulpit in which there's a Christmas box. The preacher wonders what might be inside the box and gets very excited. When the present is opened, it is empty except for a note saying, 'No present for you this Christmas – you're not worth it'. While everyone is recovering from the shock, a tele-message is brought in for the preacher. It reads:

'Got the angel's message *Stop* Sorry *Stop* Can't leave the sheep tonight *Stop* Too many wild animals about *Stop* It's just not worth the risk *Stop* Jared, Asraf and Yussuf *Stop* Shepherds'

Fine Christmas this is going to be. I'm not worth a present and the shepherds don't think it's worth coming!

A second tele-message is brought in. It reads:

'Understand new king born Bethlehem *Stop* Would come but it's an awful long way *Stop* What with winter coming on it's just not worth it *Stop* Will put gifts in the post *Stop* Best wishes Caspar, Melchior and Balthazar *Stop* Wise Men'

Well I suppose it *is* asking a lot because they do have to travel a long way – still it won't be like Christmas this year without them.

A third tele-message is brought in. It reads:

'Had second thoughts *Stop* Stables are smelly *Stop* Farm animals carry germs *Stop* Can't take the risk of being born without a doctor in attendance *Stop* Just not worth it *Stop* The Baby *Stop*'

What a dreadful Christmas! Everybody thinks it's too risky, it costs too much! It's not worth it!

Conclusion: But Christmas *was* costly. God gave himself to us because he thinks we *are* worth it. The shepherds and the wise men *did* come because Jesus *was* worth it.

➤ ➤ ➤ ➤ ➤ ➤

THE OUTSIDE OR THE INSIDE

Luke 2:1-35

Visual aids:	*Large present wrapped with many layers of paper with a wooden cross inside*

Did you get any presents? Were they wrapped in Christmas paper? How were they wrapped up? Do you like unwrapping presents? Are you like me, can't wait to get inside? Do you leave bits of wrapping paper all over the house?

I have a parcel here. Inside is what Christmas is all about, but there's lots of wrapping. Let's get some of it off and enjoy the *real* thing. (Inside the first layer is another box marked 'Mary, Joseph and the donkey'.) We all enjoy singing 'Little Donkey', but that's not what Christmas is about. It is wrapping, not present. (Inside the next layer is a box marked 'Inn, stable and manger'.) Yes, that looks better, but is it? Christmas without a crib scene wouldn't be half as lovely, but it's still just wrapping, not what Christmas is really about. (The next layer: 'sheep and shepherds'.) Very Christmassy, but still wrapping. (The next layer: 'angels'.) Is that the real present? No, it's still wrapping. (The next layer: 'the baby'.) That's not wrapping. No baby, no Christmas. But is that what Christmas is all about? There are lots of babies, but we don't celebrate their birthdays in church every year. (The next layer: 'cross'.) Well, that's a surprise. What a strange thing to say Christmas is about. A piece of wood in the form of a cross. Isn't that Good Friday? If that baby hadn't grown up and died for us to show how much God loves us, then we wouldn't be here this morning. We wouldn't be interested in Mary's baby. But we are interested and excited, not just because a baby was born, but because he was born to be our Saviour.

 # JOY

Luke 2:10

Visual aids:	*Balloons for all the children present*

Begin by talking about gifts and Jesus' birthday. Then produce some balloons with the word JOY written on them.

*J*esus first
*O*thers second
*Y*ourself last

Jesus was born to show us what God is like and to teach us what *we* should be like. We couldn't have Christmas without him. We couldn't have all the joy of Christmas without him. We are happy when we are able to give pleasure to others with our gifts and cards.

We are happy when we are given presents too.

Explain that sometimes we get it the wrong way round. We are too concerned about what we are getting, forget about other people and forget about Jesus who made Christmas possible. Point out that *YOJ* is not very happy.

At the end of the service, all the children take home a *JOY* balloon to help them get it the right way round: Jesus first, others second and ourselves last of all.

TWO ILLUSTRATED TALKS

This section presents two illustrated talks: the first looks at the meaning of Advent and the second is on meeting Christ at Christmas-tide. The graphics on pages 14 to 16 are designed for use with these talks, but they may also be suitable as overhead projector slide masters for your own presentations of the Christmas story. In which case, you may find the suggestions below on using and adapting these graphics helpful.

Suggestions:

❑ The figures can be photocopied or traced – but keep the copies provided intact, as masters.
❑ If tracing, some detail may need to be missed out.
❑ If copying, add colours by hand. When colouring acetate sheets, do so on the reverse side to keep the outlines clear and avoid rubbing off.
❑ Add orange and/or yellow rays to the star of Bethlehem and to the clouds in the shepherd scene.
❑ To get greatest flexibility, cut out and photocopy each group of figures separately then stick on to a plain sheet of paper in different combinations; then make final copies on to acetates. The figures will also look different when turned over, giving mirror images.
❑ Permanent ink pens will give the best colour. Water soluble pens allow you to wipe the slide clean and recolour to give the characters a fresh identity.
❑ Using the different groups plus the shepherds reversed, you should be able to compose:
  – angels appearing to shepherds
  – shepherds looking over Jerusalem
  – shepherds (reversed) arriving at stable
  – holy family
  – wise men looking over Jerusalem
  – wise men looking/following star
  – wise men arriving at stable
  – wise men, shepherds and holy family.

► ► ► ► ► ► # *ADVENT*

Isaiah 40:3-11

Aim:	*This will vary with the emphasis you want to place on the material. The central objective is to show that being ready is very important. Just as people had to be ready to make possible Jesus' first coming, so we are to be ready and make ready for his return.*
Visual aids:	*OHP slides are provided of four captions and three pictures of shepherds, wise men, and a family group of Mary, Joseph and the baby*
	Large Christmas card, wrapped-up present, some decorations, paper chains, baubles, etc.
	Make additional pictures of wise men, shepherds, Mary and Jesus on OHP slides by tracing alternative poses from the ones we have provided (for example, Mary and Joseph without Jesus).
	Optional: Theatre, cinema or similar poster advertising something 'coming soon'. (You can make up your own or draw on an OHP.)

Introduction

What is the meaning of Advent? When your teacher goes out of the room and tells you to get on with your work, do you get on with your work? Do you ever have someone who watches? When the teacher is coming, the watcher runs in whispering 'He's coming!' (Put up 'He's coming' on the OHP.)

Optional: I wonder how many times you have seen a poster (hold up a poster, or put up your OHP picture) about something that looks really good. It has 'Coming Soon' stamped across it. (Alternatively, you can use other illustrations relating to the life of your community or the country, about something or someone who is 'coming soon'.)

Advent is all about the coming of Jesus. But if someone or something is expected, then there's lots of preparation to be done.
I expect you're all busy preparing for Christmas. (Ask questions such as, 'How many shopping days are left?', 'What are you doing to prepare for Christmas?' Draw out activities such as sending cards and presents, making decorations, etc.)

Optional: Display cards, presents and decorations at the front of the church.

Let's think back to that very first Christmas of all. God prepared for that, not just for months, or even for years, but for thousands of years. He wanted everything to be exactly right. The Bible tells us, 'When the time was right, God sent forth his Son' (Galatians 4:4).

How did God get people ready?

❑ God began speaking to his people through the prophets. The first half of the Bible is all about what happened before Jesus came, the second half is what happened after he came. They only had this half of the Bible before Jesus (hold up an Old Testament). Yet there were plenty of promises that someone like Jesus would come.

Everyone knew. Every mother who had a little boy wondered secretly whether her son was to be the 'Messiah'. He would be coming soon.
(Put up the caption 'Coming Soon'.) In church they would hear about the coming of the Messiah. And the preachers, the prophets talked about it. An important reading was in the book of Isaiah. Isaiah told his people to prepare the way of the Lord. People who walked in darkness would see a great light. It would show them what they were doing wrong, turning them back to God (Isaiah 9:1-7).

❑ God prepared a mother for his Son. (Uncover the picture of Mary, Joseph and the baby.)

Mary was willing to be ready: 'Behold I am the handmaid of the Lord.' Joseph had to be ready to look after Mary and the special baby, which was not his.

❑ Jesus had to be ready to come and to be born in Bethlehem, as a descendant of David. He had to be 'one of us', a real person, except without ever disobeying God his Father. (You can develop the idea of his humanity and his identity with each of us.)

❑ Who else was ready that first Christmas? The wise men. They had to be ready and willing to travel to see Jesus. What if they had reckoned it was too much hard work? Suppose they hadn't bothered? They might never have known. (Put up the picture of the wise men looking out at the sky.)

❑ The shepherds had to be ready too. They could have been too frightened to go to Bethlehem. People might have laughed at their story. It was a risk to stop watching their sheep and leave them defenceless on the hills.

Are we ready?

But, you know, many people were not ready. 'He came to his own, but his own people received him not.' Jesus became the light of the world. But unfortunately many people 'loved darkness rather than light'. They refused Jesus, they wrote him off, they ignored him, and some of them plotted to kill him.

Would *you* have been ready? Would you have helped the coming Jesus? Would you have gone to see the baby Jesus?

You don't know the answer to that question, do you? But you can answer the question in another way because you do have a chance to welcome Jesus. Let me explain. (Choose one or more conclusions as appropriate.)

1. Do you know that Jesus comes to people today? He will come and be with them and live with them and help them to follow him. Have you welcomed Jesus into your life?

2. Many people don't realize that Jesus wants to come and share their lives with them. Will you help them? Will you help your friends to make ready for the coming of Jesus? Will you help them invite him in?

3. Do you know that Jesus is going to come to the world again? He is going to need people to be ready for him and to make ready for him. So you *do* have a chance to welcome Jesus. Will *you* be ready?

► ► ► ► ► ►

CHRISTMAS

Luke 2:8-20 and Matthew 2:1-12

Visual aids:	*OHP picture of shepherds in fields, OHP picture of wise men*

Introduction

Ask how many people are going away for Christmas or have visitors coming. Think about journeys and what's at the end of them.

The shepherds' journey to Jesus

Let's try in our thoughts to see what those shepherds must have felt so long ago.

(Set the scene with an OHP picture.) The shepherds were out in the fields as they'd been so many times before. It was cold. Suddenly, an angel appeared to them and the glory of the Lord shone around them.

(Put yellow-coloured overlay on OHP acetate to indicate beams of light falling on the shepherds.)

What happened? They were afraid.

(Put up caption 'afraid' on OHP.)

The angel told them not to be afraid. He brought them good news – joy to all the people. The Saviour had been born.

What did they do? They could have said, 'Let's stay here. It was only a vision. Perhaps it was our imagination. People will laugh at us. It's not really important.'

(Put up 'let's go' on the OHP.)

They could have been too afraid or doubting. They had to make a step in the right direction. God often leaves the first step of the journey to us – he gets us alert, available, but it's up to us to move on (compare Peter in prison in Acts 11).

What was at the end of their journey? Joy – they had seen and heard. They shared the good news. Isn't it great that God gave his good news to those ordinary, everyday people.

The wise men journey to Jesus

The wise men had seen the star in the east signifying the birth of the King. (Put up picture of the wise men looking out.) They came to look for him in the most obvious place, the palace of King Herod.

They could have waited until they had heard it on the news, or read it in the papers. They could have said, 'It isn't worth the bother.' But they went. They said, 'Let's go!'

(Put up 'let's go' on the OHP.)

God's plan was different. What is seemingly foolish to us is God's great plan. Once we begin to understand that God works in opposite ways to us we see his plans in a different light. So we find, as we look at the Bible, that *God didn't choose a palace in Jerusalem.* No, the prophets speak of the Messiah coming from Bethlehem.

The baby was not born in a royal palace. God as a baby was to be part of a human family, to experience pain, weariness, loneliness. 'He emptied himself.'

There was no room in the inn; even the luxury of a familiar place was denied. Jesus was born in a stable. That's how God sees kingship: he wants to meet with people in their place of need and not in an ivory tower existence.

The wise men's journey took them from luxury to poverty. They, too, came with a sense of anticipation. Perhaps they came with a sense of doubt after two years – but they kept saying, 'We have seen the star.' God had put his mark on it.

Their journey led them to joy. They presented gifts of kingship, in a humble home.

Our journey to Jesus

Perhaps it's only as we come before him in humility that we truly see him as King. Like Simeon, we are able to say, 'Here is what I've been waiting for.' It's that sort of journey we need to make as Christians, expectant that God will work, even in our doubts. We can either stay put or step out and know joy.

Jesus often asks us to do things for him. Sometimes we are afraid... but there is no need to fear. We can say: 'Let's go!'

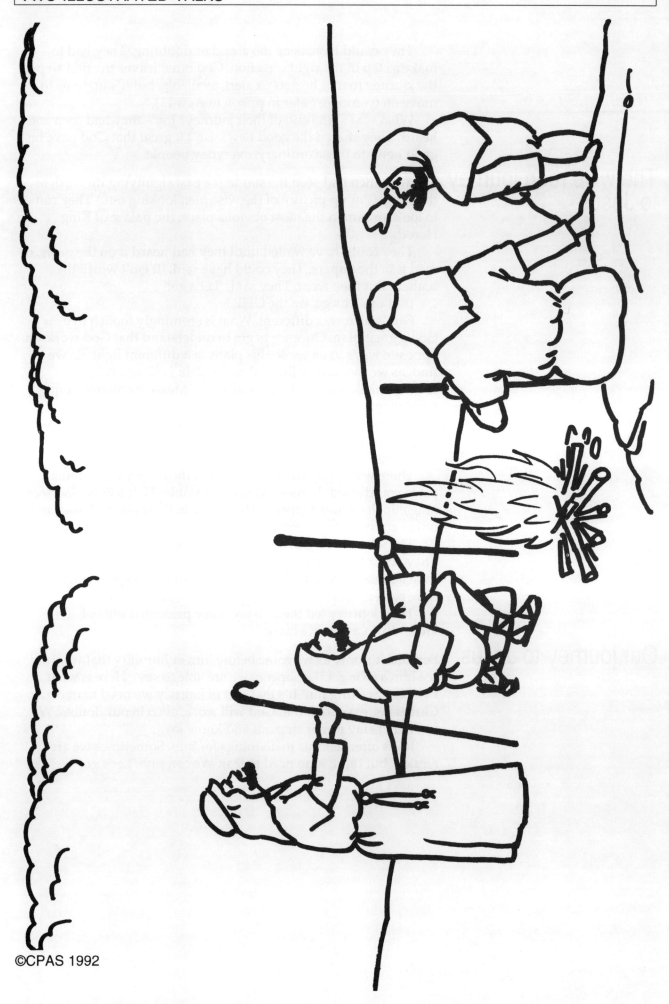

©CPAS 1992

CHRISTMAS STORIES

➤ ➤ ➤ ➤ ➤ ➤ *PAPA PANOV*

Leo Tolstoy adapted this story by Ruben Saillens which tells of an
old cobbler who dreams, on Christmas Eve, that Jesus tells him he
will come to visit him the next day. On Christmas Day, he eagerly
awaits his visitor. First he sees a sweeper, blue with cold, and
invites him in for a hot drink. Next a poor mother and her baby
are taken in and fed by the kind old man. He gives the baby a tiny
pair of shoes he once made for the child he was destined never to
have. As the day wears on, a number of beggars are fed and
warmed at Papa Panov's fire. But there is no sign of his expected
visitor. At last he falls asleep and before him passes a procession
of all the people he has helped that day, all saying, 'Did you
recognize me?' Then he heard again the voice of Jesus: 'I was a
stranger and you took me in...'

➤ ➤ ➤ ➤ ➤ ➤ *THE THREE TREES*

Three trees talk together about their dreams of what they will
become one day. The first tree desires to become a baby's cradle,
and sure enough he is made into the manger and cradles the
Christchild. The second tree longs to become a boat, and
eventually he becomes the boat of fishermen on the Sea of Galilee
and carries Jesus across the lake. The third tree doesn't know *what*
he will be. He is a lone pine tree and wonders if he will ever be
good enough for an important job. At last he is chopped down for
the most important job of all. He becomes the cross of Calvary.

*On pages 19 and 20 there are illustrations for you to display with an
overhead projector when telling these stories. Note the suggestions on
using OHP acetates on page 9. Please retain the CPAS copyright notice.*

➤ ➤ ➤ ➤ ➤ ➤ THE THREE WISHES

There was once a fisherman who caught a fish which, to his surprise, could speak. 'Throw me back into the water,' it said, 'and I will grant you three wishes.' The fisherman threw it back and ran to tell his wife what had happened. The fisherman's wife was a grumpy woman and said he was a fool. Then she said if she *really* had three wishes, she would wish to live in a big house instead of a fisherman's cottage. Immediately they were transported into a beautiful and very large house. For a while she was content, but before long she wished again, this time to live in a palace as grand as the Queen's palace. Immediately they were transported into a wonderful palace, where she lived happily for a time. At last she grew discontented again and wished for a palace as grand as God's palace. Immediately they were transported into a manger in a cowshed.

➤ ➤ ➤ ➤ ➤ ➤ BORN IN A GRAVE

A true story is told of an incident in Russia during a pogrom, when it was unsafe for a Jew to be seen anywhere in the town. A Jewish couple arrived at what was thought to be a safe house. The woman was about to give birth. There was no safe place to hide her in the house. The man of the house was a grave digger. He led the woman to a newly-dug grave. There, in the bottom of the grave, in the darkness, she gave birth to her baby, afraid to cry out in her pain lest she were discovered. She was so weak with hunger that she had no milk for her baby. His first food was the tears that flowed silently in rivulets down her breast.

➤ ➤ ➤ ➤ ➤ ➤ PEACE AT CHRISTMAS

On Christmas Day 1914, during the First World War, while the Germans and the Allied armies faced each other in France, someone began singing the carol 'Silent Night, Holy Night'. A hush fell over the battlefield.

Soldiers on both sides laid down their arms, climbed out of their trenches and met together. Men who had spent weeks trying to kill each other now embraced, sang and exchanged souvenirs and cigarettes. Even a football match was organized...

And then, on 26 December, they went back to their trenches once again to kill each other.

©CPAS 1992

SEED IDEAS

►►►►►► *CHRISTMAS HOUSEPARTY*

In a church with many overseas people and those living on their own, try arranging a Christmas houseparty over the Christmas period itself. Catering can be provided, or a self-catering centre could also be successful. This venture would be very much appreciated by many for whom Christmas would be a difficult time.

►►►►►► *CHRISTMAS CONCERT*

A concert could be held on the Saturday afternoon before Christmas. Try an hour-and-a-half programme of Christmas music – both spiritual and secular – performed by the robed choir and music group, giving a balance of taste. Items could be linked by the minister acting as compere, thus giving opportunity for a short, pithy input on Christian issues. Make it a mixture of the serious and the jolly – and end with 'Jingle Bells'. It should draw in a number of 'fringers', who wouldn't usually come to a Sunday event.

►►►►►► *CRIB SERVICE*

Hold a crib service in the late afternoon of Christmas Eve lasting for about three quarters of an hour. The service could consist of putting the figures in the crib, well-known carols, a very short talk based on the Christmas story, and some prayers. Try, as the main attraction, a procession of children round the church following the star (we have an electronically operated gadget which flashes!). The church should be packed out. There will be total chaos and it will be very noisy, but there's a magic about it. It will also draw in lots of parents who are not usually seen during the rest of the year.

➤ ➤ ➤ ➤ ➤ ➤ CHRISTMAS EVE SERVICE

A service at 5.00pm on Christmas Eve is very user-friendly, especially when parents are at their wits' end and looking forward to getting the kids somewhere else. Make the service last for a maximum of thirty minutes and concentrate on the story of Christmas which the majority of the children don't know. Serve tea, orange juice, mince pies and chocolate log after the service.

➤ ➤ ➤ ➤ ➤ ➤ MEDIEVAL SERVICE

Let everyone dress up in medieval costumes to enact the Christmas story in a revamped mystery play. Being in the play enables the story to take people by surprise in a new way.

➤ ➤ ➤ ➤ ➤ ➤ FLOWERS FOR CHRISTMAS

With the church decorated for Christmas, invite people to come in during three afternoons before Christmas Eve to spend time looking at the decorations and be quiet. A team of people from the church could be available to pray for people as appropriate. We carried out this exercise in a large urban area, and it attracted some 200 to 300 people. It seemed to give substance to the claim that many people welcome Christmas as an excuse for coming into church. Bringing the children in to see the decorations was a way many found of taking advantage of this offer.

➤ ➤ ➤ ➤ ➤ ➤ MIDNIGHT CELEBRATION

At traditional midnight Communion services, many who come are clearly not familiar with the service and appear to be slightly embarrassed. Yet they obviously want to come to church late at night on Christmas Eve. Try a different form of service which contains the traditional blend of carols, a few readings, some drama, and a short re-telling of the Christmas story with its significance and relevance underlined. Do not include Holy Communion. Some church members may object to losing their midnight service, but the majority will be delighted that so many strangers come, feel at home, and clearly appreciate the event.

➤ ➤ ➤ ➤ ➤ ➤ ## *TRADITIONAL SERVICES*

These events still have a considerable attraction. Doing them as well as you possibly can is one way of obtaining packed services. An address explaining the meaning of Christmas, and giving people the opportunity to respond to its message by taking booklets, may be met with considerable response. Try giving out free copies of J. John's *What's the Point of Christmas?* by Lion Publishing.

➤ ➤ ➤ ➤ ➤ ➤ ## *CHRISTMAS CABARET*

Try this idea for non-Christian, housebound people. The programme might consist of a variety of games and sketches, prefaced by an excellent lunch. A brief talk given by a gifted communicator makes the event enjoyable and worthwhile. Our tradition is to hold this on New Year's Day in comfortable surroundings. Transport is provided.

➤ ➤ ➤ ➤ ➤ ➤ ## *CHRISTMAS GUEST SUPPER*

Set out your church lounge in restaurant-style with tables (for two, four and six) booked in advance. Create the atmosphere with candles, background music and waiter service. Follow the meal with a musical and dramatic presentation with modern and traditional songs but no separate talk. The time taken (apart from the meal) should be about forty minutes. The evening should be for church members provided they bring non-church friends as guests. We found such an evening was widely welcomed, and gave the chance for conversation and discussion at the tables in a non-threatening way about the true meaning of Christmas.

➤ ➤ ➤ ➤ ➤ ➤ ## *ADVENT TEAS*

In an area where there are a number of retired people, often living on their own, teas might be organized for the four Sundays of Advent. Invite people into church members' homes where a special tea has been provided. Make Advent candles and crowns the focus of decoration on the meal table and conclude the event with a reading and prayer. The purpose of the teas is to give some practical expression of concern to those who are living alone, to provide an enjoyable time when a few people, generally neighbours, can be together, and to invite those attending to come to church for one of the Christmas services. The whole enterprise needs to be centrally co-ordinated with hosts having adequate flexibility to adjust the food and programme to suit their own homes and the guests' needs.

➤ ➤ ➤ ➤ ➤ ➤ CHRISTMAS LUNCH

Try organizing a lunch for all those who would otherwise be spending Christmas on their own. Immediately after the end of the main service invite these guests to go along to the nearby rectory, have a pre-lunch drink, and sit down to a traditional Christmas dinner. We found people stayed until mid-afternoon, and they were then taken home. Twenty people responded initially. As numbers grew, the event was transferred to the well-equipped church centre. No charge was made, the costs being covered by the rector, but so many members of the congregation voluntarily contributed that the rector was left with a surplus!

➤ ➤ ➤ ➤ ➤ ➤ CHRISTINGLE

Christingle services are very popular and widely used. With care it can be an excellent tool to help people understand and appreciate Christmas that little bit more.

➤ ➤ ➤ ➤ ➤ ➤ STUDENTS' NEW YEAR MEETING

Provide a buffet meal for students about to go up to college for the winter term. We found the evening provided for an exchange of news, prayer and encouragement.

➤ ➤ ➤ ➤ ➤ ➤ ALTERNATIVE CAROL SERVICE

The Alternative Carol Service is an event made up almost entirely of modern music, together with drama, dance and mime. This should be in addition to the traditional Christmas services held at other times.

➤ ➤ ➤ ➤ ➤ ➤ *EPIPHANY PARTY*

This is specifically designed to invite people who once attended local churches but no longer do so. Ours took place in an urban priority area. A card and letter was taken round to a large number of people with the invitation for them to come to the carol service and start again. A large number responded and some returned to active church membership. Epiphany and New Year themes were combined for the service.

➤ ➤ ➤ ➤ ➤ ➤ *FOR THOSE WHO FIND CHRISTMAS DIFFICULT*

A programme of events might be organized to include such things as walks, musical evenings, children and young people's activities. Informal invitations are made by the members of the congregations, and they advertise times when clergy could be available. Ours is an annual programme attempting to reach out to the large number of people – not those who are on their own – who find Christmas time difficult.

➤ ➤ ➤ ➤ ➤ ➤ *CHILDREN'S VISITS TO RESIDENTIAL HOMES*

Groups of children, aged approximately seven to ten years, could visit residential homes in the parish to sing and offer a small play with readings. It will be enormously appreciated by the residents and staff. It evokes memories of Christmas long ago, and gives adult helpers the chance to talk and pray with residents.

➤ ➤ ➤ ➤ ➤ ➤ *THE DRAMATISED BIBLE*

The new edition of selected readings from *The Dramatised Bible* provides plenty of resources for reading at Advent, Christmas and Epiphany.

The Dramatised Bible and Dramatised Bible Readings for Festivals are published by Bible Society/Marshalls and are available from CPAS Sales (0926 334242).

➤ ➤ ➤ ➤ ➤ ➤

HELP FOR THE HOMELESS

Organize a small group of people to staff soup kitchens and let secular and Christian groups make sleeping provisions. It will provide a good challenge for the congregation to contribute something specific to those outside of their usual contacts, and will prove to be a powerful education tool about those in such circumstances.

➤ ➤ ➤ ➤ ➤ ➤

CHILDREN AND YOUNG PEOPLE'S ACTIVITY CLUBS

Since the post-Christmas period is often a time when many children, young people and families are not sure what to do, try arranging a series of day activities. They will be very welcome and profitable. Residential and non-residential programmes could be organized over several years. They could be linked to Confirmation training and follow-up, or designed to include some young people who are usually away at school or college. And other times they might be designed simply to give a balance of Christian teaching and recreation. Walks, outings, discussion, projects, visits and helping others might all be part of the programme. Good advance warning gives parents the chance to organize family visits outside holiday club dates.

➤ ➤ ➤ ➤ ➤ ➤

PARISH PARTY PROVIDED BY THE YOUNG PEOPLE

This high-risk activity(!) could prove a huge success. Ask the young people to organize the whole evening, concluding with some lighthearted sketches and some closing comments as to what Christmas means to the young people themselves.
An alternative focus could be a party, again organized by the youth fellowship, for local senior citizens. Musical recitals and readings by the young people can be linked with cards and maybe a quiz based on old slides of the locality (ask at the library for these).

➤ ➤ ➤ ➤ ➤ ➤ # *CHRISTMAS MUSIC*

Among the abundance of music available for Christmas are *Carols for Today*, *Carol Praise*, *Play Carol Praise* and *Carolling*, all produced by Jubilate. *Carols for Today* is for choirs. *Carol Praise* contains a wider variety of music styles, and *Play Carol Praise* is marvellous for developing small orchestras.

These books are available from CPAS Sales (0926 334242).

➤ ➤ ➤ ➤ ➤ ➤ # *ADVENT WREATH*

Advent wreaths could be made with places for five candles, one for each Sunday of Advent and the centre place for Christmas Day itself. Members of the congregation could be encouraged to make one for their own home and light a new candle for each Sunday lunch. A bigger one could then be made for the church. Some of the family ones could be made in children's groups at an evening workshop to which parents are invited. The large one for the church could be made by the youth group.

BANNERS FOR CHRISTMAS

The aim of these notes is to provide a few ideas for Christmas banners for those who would like to make them, but who don't know where to begin. The notes may also be useful for those who are already banner-makers, to encourage them to continue this very worthwhile 'silent ministry' of proclaiming God's Word.

What is seen is much more readily remembered than what is heard, so here is an opportunity to show to those around us the true meaning of Christmas.

Where do good ideas come from?

❑ The Bible. Re-read the Christmas story in the Gospels of Matthew and Luke (and John 1 and Philippians 2).
❑ Books of carols, old and new.
❑ Books on 'Christmas customs', 'Things to do at Christmas', 'Poems for Christmas', etc.
❑ Christmas cards.

Pray for inspiration. Write down any thoughts or words that you find helpful. Translate these ideas into drawings. How can you best depict joy, glory, peace, light, love?

Think through what Christmas means for you, your family, your group or your church.

Look at adverts, posters and books on lettering to get ideas for the style of the words that might be suitable.

Design

The keynote is simplicity. Keep your design simple and do away with any fussy details. A simple banner, well made, will have much more immediate impact than a very detailed one. You want people to get the message 'at a glance'.

Lettering

Make sure it will be clearly seen from the back of your church. Take time to get the size right.

Background material

Choose a good, closely-woven fabric; it will keep its shape better. Experiment to find which colours are most suitable in the situation where the banner will hang. Good lighting is essential.

Fabrics

Felt is available in an excellent range of colours. It is easy to use, does not fray, and is suitable for many designs. But do choose the best you can afford as the quality varies considerably. Variation in texture can be obtained with corded fabric, velvet, chiffon and many other fabrics and yarns. Iron-on Vilene is useful for backing fabrics that fray. If a 3-D effect is required, use a little terylene wadding for padding. Gold and silver fabrics bring a brightness and sparkle to banners and are especially good for use at Christmas.

Making the banner

The usual methods of appliqué are suitable for sewing motifs to the background fabric. Matching, contrasting or invisible threads may be used, and sometimes cord or narrow braid is useful for outlining a design. Alternatively, machine 'zigzag' stitching could be used.

Sticking is possible instead of stitching. For general use, a PVA adhesive is excellent, used neat or diluted. It dries to a clear film and does not discolour with age. 'Uhu' and 'Pritt', (non-stringing), are also very good. Always test glues on a sample of fabric first. When the design has been completed, line the banner to neaten the back. This will also make it hang better. Leave channels at the top and bottom for rod and your banner is ready for use.

Getting started

To start you off, there are a few designs for Christmas banners included. They are in a variety of styles: traditional, modern, words only, and in assorted sizes.

Note: line drawings from the *Good News Bible* may be used if prior permission is obtained from the Bible Society, Stonehill Green, Westlea, Swindon, SN5 7BR.

For books with more ideas and tips on making banners, see the reference booklist on page 48.

CHRIST IS HERE

JESUS

SON OF GOD

The Light of Christ has come into the world

PEACE

LOVE

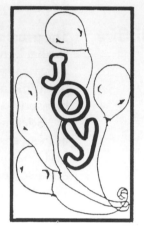

JOY

WELCOME JESUS

BORN TODAY

GLORY to GOD

in the highest

GLORY TO GOD

PEACE ON EARTH

JOY

to the world

CHRIST

has come

EMMANUEL

COME and WORSHIP CHRIST

the new-born King

GOOD NEWS !

THE SAVIOUR IS HERE

COME Let us adore Him

CHRIST THE LORD

EMMANUEL GOD IS WITH US

GLORY TO THE NEW-BORN KING

LOVE PEACE

Love came down at Christmas

DRAMA SKETCHES

➤ ➤ ➤ *NO ROOM*

Landlord in pulpit. Enter two men: Amos and Joseph.

Amos: What a fuss and bother all this is! Who does this fella Caesar think he is anyway, making half the country leave home and travel miles, just to get their names in a book?

Barnabas: He's a business man, that's what. Wants to make sure we're paying him enough tax money.

Landlord: Come on, gentlemen, you're the last ones. *(Holds up hand to approaching Joseph and Mary)* Sorry, sir, absolutely no more room. We're crammed full as it is.

Joseph: But my wife is expecting.

Landlord: I'm sorry but I can't squeeze another person in here. If you're really desperate you can use the cowshed over there. No charge for a cowshed! *(Laughs and goes off)*

Amos: Whew, we were lucky! I don't fancy a filthy cowshed tonight.

Barnabas: I'm sorry for that young couple. The girl's expecting a baby. Looks as if she's near her time too. Looks worn out.

Amos: *(Sarcastically)* What about my good friend Barnabas giving up his bed?

Barnabas: Me? Not likely! I love myself too much.

Amos: *(Forlornly)* That's the trouble. We all love ourselves too much. Sometimes I wish I could be saved from myself – you know, start all over again.

Barnabas: You'll be getting all religious next – like that lot that talk about God promising to send a Saviour.

Amos: Huh! Well, if he did promise to help us he must have forgotten all about it. It's 700 years since the prophets were on about that. Come on, I'm off to bed.

Barnabas: Good idea.

The two men exit. Shepherds come on running up the central aisle. They stop at the chancel steps and then continue. The stable is a structure in front of the communion table, with its lighting on a dimmer switch.

1st shepherd:	Look, there's a light in the cowshed. That will be the place.
2nd shepherd:	Now calm down. We'll scare the living daylights out of 'em if we rush in like this.
1st shepherd:	I feel all of a dither. Fancy God telling us first. I've never seen an angel before – my legs feel like jelly.
2nd shepherd:	Never mind your legs. Come on – quietly does it.

Shepherds exit. The two men enter, yawning and looking around.

Barnabas:	Bethlehem looks better by day, doesn't it? Nice little place. And you know, that was the best night's sleep I've had in years.
Amos:	Mmm, don't think I slept a wink. Don't know what it was; strange bed perhaps. I kept feeling something odd was happening. At one point I thought I saw angels coming from over those hills and singing.
Barnabas:	Singing? In the middle of the night? Reckon you had too much goat's cheese for supper!

Shepherds rush in.

Shepherds:	Have you heard the news?
Men:	What news? Don't tell us Caesar cancelled the census and we've heard nothing.
1st shepherd:	No! Nothing like that. Far more important! It's fantastic – right here in Bethlehem! In our town.
Men:	What's happened?
2nd shepherd:	God's Saviour! After 700 years. He was born last night. Didn't you hear the singing?
Amos:	Singing, did you say? I did hear singing. *(Turns to Barnabas indignantly)* And it wasn't goat's cheese for supper!
1st shepherd:	We saw them! Hundreds of angels singing, and the one that spoke said, 'I am bringing you the good news that the promised Saviour has been born tonight and you will find him lying in a manger.'
Amos:	*(Startled)* In a manger? In a cowshed? God born in a cowshed? *(Turns to Barnabas)* By gum – it was that young couple. You know, the girl there was no room for last night!
Barnabas:	The ones we wouldn't give up our beds for.
Amos:	Oh no! If I'd only known. God's promised Messiah at last and I slept comfy in the pub and let him be born in a cowshed. Sinful, selfish wretch that I am. *(Holds head in hands)*
1st shepherd:	The baby's father said he was going to be called Jesus because he would save his people from their sins.

2nd shepherd:	*(Slaps Amos on back)* Friend, a Saviour is good news! It means God wants to forgive. It means we've got the chance to start all over again.
Amos:	A fresh start did you say? That's what I need! Jesus, I'd give up my bed for you now.
1st shepherd:	*(To audience)* Watch out world. Jesus will make a new man of him.
Barnabas:	*(Scratching head)* Maybe it wasn't goat's cheese after all.

➤ ➤ ➤ *THE SPECIAL OFFER*

This drama illustrates the lengths people will go to in order to obtain a 'special offer' – something they think is good value. After the drama apply it to Christmas. Jesus is the greatest offer that God could ever make to us. How much do we want to have what God has offered? How much are we prepared to put ourselves out?

Craig is seated in a shop doorway with a sleeping bag, picnic stove, etc. A group of boys come past and notice him there.

George:	What on earth are you doing there, Craig?
Craig:	Waiting for the 'Big Sale'.
Kenneth:	But it doesn't start until after Christmas.
Craig:	I know, but I wanted to be first in the queue.
William:	Why?
Craig:	To get the snooker table.
Kenneth:	The one in the window?
Craig:	That's right. It's the star bargain. Only £50 – it must be worth ten times that.
William:	And the rest!
George:	Will you get it?
Craig:	Well, I'll be first through the door, and I found out exactly what to do once I'm inside.
Kenneth:	But you'll have to stay here all week!
Craig:	Yes.
George:	Night and day?
Craig:	All the time. It'll be really mellow!

George:	Really freezing, you mean! It's the middle of winter.
Craig:	I've got a special sleeping bag and a foil blanket, so I should be OK.
William:	What about food?
Craig:	Mum and Sis' are going to bring me hot meals – Sis' thinks I'm mad! And I've got a stove so I can make hot drinks.
Kenneth:	But what about going – you know... *(Breaks off, embarrassed)*
Craig:	Toilet, you mean? *(All giggle)*
Kenneth:	Yeah. You'll have to go sometime!
Craig:	Of course. Terry, my big brother, says he'll stand guard over my place when I have to go – I've had to promise to let him use the table sometimes. And the local policeman said he'd stop anyone from grabbing my place.
George:	What about at night?
Craig:	Oh, the security guard'll be there then.
William:	Well, you've certainly got it all organized.
Kenneth:	Won't you get fed up? It'll be awfully boring.
George:	You'll miss all the holiday programmes on TV!
Craig:	Can't be helped. But I'm determined to have the snooker table.
William:	You really want it, don't you? I couldn't do what you're doing.
Craig:	You could, if you wanted it as badly as I do!
Kenneth:	Good luck, then. We'll visit you every day. Won't we, lads?
George and William:	Yeah.
Craig:	Great!
William:	If we do, will you let us have a go on your table?
Craig:	Of course! I won't be able to play properly on my own, will I?
George:	Hey, guys – let's see if any of the other stores are giving anything away!

All exit, except Craig.

➤ ➤ ➤ *BORN TO DIE*

The aim of this drama is to leap forward, through the shepherds' conversation, from Jesus' birth to his death as the Lamb of God. Use this as an evangelistic starting point.

3 Shepherds – teenage son, middle-aged father and Another.

Son:	It's so dull out here in the hills, watching the sheep. Nothing ever happens.
Father:	Well, son, it did once. Angels filled the whole sky. I'll never forget.
Son:	Oh I know, father, all about the baby in the cowshed. But that was donkeys' years ago, before I was born. I've never seen an angel.
Another:	What happened to the baby afterwards?
Father:	I don't know. Probably he died that awful night when Herod's soldiers surrounded Bethlehem and killed all the babies.
Son:	Wasn't he supposed to be the Messiah? Surely God wouldn't let him be killed?
Father:	Maybe not. Perhaps they got away. We tried to find out but no one was sure.
Another:	How long ago was it? If he did escape how old would he be now?
Father:	I was a youngster then. Yes it must be... thirty years or more.
Son:	Surely we'd have heard of him now, if he is alive?
Another:	Strange, you know. There was a lot of 'Messiah talk' going on in Jerusalem when I went in for Passover. It was all about a man called Jesus of Nazareth.
Son:	The Messiah won't come from Nazareth. He will come from Bethlehem.
Father:	But the baby we saw didn't really belong to Bethlehem. His parents had come for the census and the baby was born there. *(Thoughtfully)* Jesus is a common name – but it means 'Saviour'. The angels said he was our Saviour... Did you see him?
Another:	Yes, on Sunday. There was a great crowd cheering and waving branches. I just caught a glimpse of Jesus – an ordinary man on a donkey. But the priests didn't like the people shouting 'Son of David'. I'm sure they'll try to get rid of him.
Son:	They couldn't kill the Messiah! *(Pause)*
Father:	I'm not sure. There's a strange verse in Scripture about God's servant being 'led like a lamb to the slaughter'. We know what it feels like to watch our lambs being taken away to be killed. *(Pause)*
Son:	*(Standing)* Dawn's breaking. It's Friday morning.
Another:	The Passover lambs will be sacrificed today.
Son:	Poor lambs. Born to die.

➤ ➤ ➤   *A MIME FOR INFANTS*

The advantage of a mime is that the children do not have to learn words. The words read by the four 'voices' should be audible (amplified if necessary) and well practised. Carols are optional. If you use them, the presentation becomes long enough to make a service on its own.

Carol:	'Once in royal David's city'

(During the carol the nativity tableau – shepherds, wise men, innkeeper, angels, Mary and Joseph – is formed near the chancel steps. Children sit and kneel facing the scene.)

1st voice: Once again, as Christmas draws near, we see a familiar sight. Look! there at the centre of it all is Jesus: a tiny baby in a far-off land, put there by our heavenly Father to be our Saviour.

There, too, is his mother, Mary – with Joseph nearby to care for them both.

There are shepherds from the nearby hills and the kindly innkeeper. God has sent angels all glorious and splendid. Wise men from far-off lands have come with gifts.

And look again, there are children there who have come to gaze and wonder.

Carol: 'Infant holy, infant lowly'

1st voice: Let us speak to them and ask them why they are here.

2nd voice: Children! You gaze at this lovely sight. Do you know why you are here? Do you understand what it all means?

Perhaps, who knows, you understand better than anyone else in the world... Perhaps there are things you do not yet fully know... Draw back a little. Yes. Make room and you shall hear again the whole wonderful story. *(The children stand and withdraw to nearby seats)*

2nd voice: I see wise men with gifts. How came you to this place? Why did you come? What is your part in the story? *(The wise men step forward)*

3rd voice: As we studied the wisdom of our nations, a star appeared in the sky guiding us here and showing that a king was to be born in this place, a king with all wisdom and power. So we bring our gifts as befits a king: gold, frankincense and myrrh. *(The wise men move to nearby seats)*

1st voice: Thank you, wise men. Now, shepherds, you are rough and simple men; should you be here amid all this splendour? What is your story? *(The shepherds move forward)*

3rd voice: Why yes! We are rough and simple as you so rightly say. But while we were at our humble task of guarding our sheep on the cold hillside, we were astonished by this band of shining angels! Straight from heaven they had come with a message for our ears alone. And a summons! And a sign! We left our sheep and found this place as the angels said we must. I think somehow that God chose us because we were rough and simple. His ways are sometimes hard for us to understand. But we have been glad to be here and feel we must tell the others what we have seen. *(Shepherds withdraw. Angels move forward)*

All voices: Glory be to God on high, and on earth peace and good will towards men.

Carol: 'Hark! The herald angels sing'

(Angels and shepherds make their own tableau. As the carol ends they withdraw to their seats. The innkeeper steps forward.)

2nd voice: Are you the innkeeper? I feel sure you are. You have a part in this story I know. Please tell us about it.

3rd voice: I feel ashamed, to tell you the truth. If I had known who these holy and blessed travellers were, I would have tried to do better. This is a good inn with a good name, but we were so busy you see. And so crowded. It would have been wrong to turn others out of their rooms even if they would have gone. But a stable! For these! I would have done anything had I only known. *(Joseph steps forward with Mary)*

4th voice: Do not fret, good innkeeper. You played the part that God had planned. You heard how the shepherds said that his ways are beyond our simple understanding. God needed your stable tonight, not your finest rooms. This stable will come to be known down the long years as the holiest place on the whole wide earth. We came from Nazareth, you made us welcome, and we are thankful.

Carol: 'Mary was watching tenderly'

2nd voice: Now children, once more the tale is told and you may return to gaze again at the Infant Redeemer, your brother, friend and Saviour. Come I say, draw near and see again what Christmas means.

1st voice: Come close. Here is the heart and the meaning of all things. The centre of Christmas and the centre of the world. *(The whole tableau reforms)*

Carol: 'Girls and boys, leave your toys'

A Christmas Benediction

➤ ➤ ➤ *PREPARING FOR CHRISTMAS*

It has begun. The hurly-burly of preparations; the making of cakes and puddings; the aching hands and feet; the anxious search for presents.

Is this how it should be, Lord?

Father, we call a halt. Here, and now, and at this moment. And we think of the first Christmas when history paused and turned upon its hinges as your Son became a man, born into the family of working parents, born to experience everything for us – and even to bear our sins.

Help each one of us to prepare for Christmas by finding time for quiet, time to drink in the wonder and beauty of your Son's birth, time to offer again our hearts and each part of our life to him.

May the pages of our diary turn upon this silent hinge. May our work be rooted and grounded in peace.

Jesus said, 'My peace I give to you, but not the sort the world gives.'

Father, we understand only too well the kind of peace which mankind manufactures: the peace of political and other settlements. Give to more and more of us all over the world the peace we do not understand, the peace which passes understanding, the peace which flows from unconditional obedience to the law of love, give us your kind of peace. And we pray for those in positions of power, authority and influence, that they may open their hearts and give their wills to you, that you may work through them.

Jesus said, 'When you give food or drink to someone who has none, you're giving it to me.'

Save us, Father, from becoming hardened to the numerous pleas for help we see in the press each day. Open our eyes and pockets to the needs of our world. Re-organize our hearts so that it may not be a burden to give but a relief.

Jesus said, 'Man cannot live by bread alone.'

Dear Lord, the giver of all, guide our giving so that we may support all those who spend their lives, at home and all over the world, feeding the spirit of man with the good news of Christmas.

Father, with all our hearts we thank you for all that you have given us through Jesus Christ our Lord.

To your Name, Lord Jesus, help me to
bow the knee and all its worshipping;
bow the head and all its thinking;
bow the will and all its choosing;
bow the heart and all its loving,
today, tomorrow, and all the days of my life. Amen.

➤ ➤ ➤ *CHRISTMAS THEN AND NOW*

This reading needs two voices.

In the beginning there was a pregnant girl – not married – who said she had seen an angel. Joseph didn't believe her. Would you? But after God spoke to him he had to change his mind.

In the end there are no doubts, no questions. There's no mystery of God becoming man, only commercial certainty and empty messages of goodwill delivered by post.

In the beginning there was a homeless couple. Usual sort of government idea – make everyone go somewhere difficult in winter to fill in forms. There was no midwife, no maternity ward, no bed. Only a stable.

In the end there are glossy pictures of her with tidy animals and neat angels. No problems – 10 copies for 50p. No pain, no dirt, no obedience to the will of God.

In the beginning the baby became a refugee because the tyrant, Herod, was so scared that he killed all the baby boys. The mothers all cried, but don't let's be miserable at Christmas.

In the end the tears are of the lonely and the homeless, who wait for Christmas to be over.

In the beginning the baby grew up and his parents didn't understand him. He upset their friends by talking about God and wanting to change things.

In the end people hope God will not upset the fun at Christmas. It's nice to mention him, but please don't let him come and change things.

In the beginning the baby grew up and was tortured to death very slowly because he said men should come close to God through him. He said God would set them free from fear and hate and feeling unloved and would make them whole if they would follow him.

In the end mankind often chooses fear and hate and feeling unloved, thinking and saying that this is freedom.

In the beginning God made the world.

In the end man will unmake the world. The story about God dying for men is either true or a terrible lie. The story about him being born in Bethlehem is either true or a terrible lie. If it is true then he wants your love.

In the beginning God makes a world...

In the end he remakes it.

ADVENT PARTY

Timetable

Why not avoid one more party close to Christmas and have an Advent Party instead? The times here are obviously adjustable to suit local requirements, but the party needs to take place when it is dark to get the full impact of the theme 'light'.

5.30pm   *Arrivals.* The hall is lit by candlelight alone. Take care not to let the children touch the candles or blow them out. As they arrive they search for six parcels which are hidden around the hall and then kept, unopened, until later in the evening.

5.45pm   *Eat* by candlelight

6.15pm   *Activities, various.* In the case of St Andrew's, the 8-11 year olds spent the time wrapping up gifts they had made previously as Christmas presents. The under-8s made cardboard candles in another room.

6.30pm   *Country dancing* or similar

6.45pm   *Unwrapping parcels together* (see below) followed by some singing, and then farewell.

Learning about Advent

You will need six parcels wrapped up and hidden around the room. The parcels need to contain the following:

Parcel 1   A 'Good News' box with enough sweets inside for one per child, and a card which says, 'Advent means good news'.

Parcel 2   A candlestick, candle, box of matches, and a card which says 'The people who walked in darkness have seen a great light' (Isaiah 9:2).

Parcel 3   A star and a small model of a baby in a manger.

Parcel 4   A New Testament with a bookmark marking John 1:5. On the bookmark is written 'Emmanuel – Jesus'.

Parcel 5   A small cross and a crown.

Parcel 6   Two pieces of card about ten inches square. On one there is a picture of a person looking sad and cowering in a dark corner; on the other a person jumping for joy in bright sunlight.

The leader's parts can be shared among however many leaders you have, and could even be done by one leader if you work alone.

Leader 1: Now we will open the packages and see what they can tell us about Advent. *(Opens parcel 1)*

Leader 2: Ooh! Good News! Lovely! *(Takes box and shakes it)* There is something inside. *(Opens box)* Great! Sweets! Toffees! Let's share them around. Oh, look, here is a card. What does it say? 'Advent means good news.' Well, yes, Advent is good news. In fact, Advent means 'coming'. Who is coming? I wonder! Come on, let's see what is in the next parcel.

Leader 3: *(Opens parcel 2. Reads aloud and sounds a bit disappointed)* What does it mean? *(Reads verse again)* We have been in the darkness tonight. I couldn't see very well at first. Imagine if it had been completely dark, we wouldn't have seen anything at all, would we? What is this 'great light' that the Bible is speaking about? *(Unwraps candle, puts it in the candlestick and lights it)* There is something very lovely about the light. Even one little candle is quite bright when everything else is dark. The people who walked in darkness were, according to Isaiah, to see a great light. These words were written in Old Testament times and referred to the coming of Jesus who was the great light many years later. Jesus himself said, 'I am the light.'

Leader 4: *(Opens parcel 3)* Here is something else which lights up the sky. *(Holds up the star)* A star of light led the wise men to Jesus. *(Holds up baby in manger)*

Leader 5: *(Opens parcel 4)* Oh! A New Testament and a bookmark. What place is it marking? *(Opens Bible and reads John 1:5)* Another Bible verse speaking about light. This time the words are in the New Testament – written after Jesus had come. Remember, 'Advent' means 'coming'. He had in fact been born, lived, died and risen again by the time these words were written. What is this written on the bookmark? 'Emmanuel – Jesus'. Jesus is Emmanuel which means 'God is with us'. Isn't it wonderful that God had this plan? He left all the glory of heaven and entered into the dark world so that we might see him.

Leader 6: *(Opens parcel 5)* People at the time of Jesus thought that he was just an ordinary baby. Some knew who he really was: 'God with us' – God himself. Mary and Joseph knew; a few shepherds knew and so did some wise men. 'Advent' we know, means 'coming'. When God came the first time he came as a baby. But God's plan is that he will come again a second time. Nobody knows when that will be, but we do know that when he comes again he will come as our king *(Puts on the crown)* and will gather together all who love him into his kingdom.

Leader 1: *(Opens the last parcel. Takes a picture of the cowering person and holds it up)* A Christian is a person who loves Jesus and has been forgiven for all his sins. A Christian has deliberately stepped out of 'darkness' into the kingdom of light *(Holds up the picture of the joyful person)* and remembers with great joy the coming of Jesus as a baby. But a Christian also looks forward with great joy to Jesus coming again as king. To find the parcels you had to search for them. It was quite dark in parts. Our world has a lot of darkness in it. If we want to find Jesus we have to look, but when we find him, he will bring more and more light into our life.

CELEBRATING WITH UNDER FIVES

▶▶▶▶▶▶ *THE GIVING OF GIFTS*

The visit of the wise men to the baby Jesus is recorded in Matthew 2:1-12. Over the centuries the Christian church has celebrated this famous visit on Twelfth Night, 6 January, so there is a good historical reason for leaving this story until after Christmas. It also gives a good opportunity to talk about giving presents slightly separated from the extravagance of Christmas Day. As well as that, it is a great story and activity with which to start a new term in your toddler group.

This retelling of a Christmas Bible story for under fives is one of a number of CPAS Bible stories and activities from *Celebrating the Festivals*. The following songs might be appropriate to keep the children's attention:

'The Virgin Mary had a baby boy'
'Lord we come to worship you'
'Two little eyes'
'Head and shoulders knees and toes'

The following visual aids will help you as you tell the story:

☆ a large star
☆ children dressed up as wise men with gifts or wise men puppets

Tell the story

Ask the children what gifts they gave at Christmas. Play a game of matching gifts to people. Have four large cards each bearing a picture of an easily-recognized type of person, e.g. a mum, a grandad, a child, someone very sporty. On some other large cards have pictures of the kind of present that would be appropriate for each of them, and allow two presents per person, e.g. a pair of slippers for grandad, some building blocks for the child, etc. Instead of pictures, you could use the real thing. The children have to say who they would give the presents to.

Story   Now tell the story of the wise men. If the children are helping you to tell the story, you will need to write down some notes for the necessary movements. Give them their instructions as you are telling the story, and ask one of the mums to 'stage direct' them.
- ❑ the wise men see the star and prepare to follow it
- ❑ the long journey
- ❑ they visit Herod (leave out with very small children)
- ❑ they find Mary, Joseph, and baby Jesus
- ❑ they kneel in worship and offer gifts

Make a wise man with a gift

Prepare in advance
- ❑ Have the outline wise man with gift photocopied on to card (p.44).
- ❑ Cut out wise man, and score along lines.
- ❑ In card, cut out templates for wise man's coat, crown, face, hands and hair, front and back (p.45).
- ❑ In rich coloured sticky paper cut out one coat per wise man.
- ❑ In pink sticky paper cut out one face and one pair of hands per wise man.
- ❑ In black/brown sticky paper cut out one pair of hair fronts and backs per wise man.
- ❑ In silver/gold sticky paper cut out two crowns per wise man.
- ❑ If you are using crayons to colour the wise man in, just photocopy him on to the card. You don't need to prepare the shapes.

Get the room ready   Put out for each child/parent:
- ❑ 1 wise man with gift
- ❑ 1 wise man's coat
- ❑ 1 wise man's face
- ❑ 1 pair of hands
- ❑ 1 front and back of hair
- ❑ 1 crown (2 pieces)

Put out on the table:
- ❑ crayons (if needed)
- ❑ PVA glue and spreaders
- ❑ pencils

What each child/parent does:
- ❑ If colouring in: with printed side up, colour in hands, coat, hair back and crown. Turn over and colour in face, hair front and crown.
- ❑ If using sticky paper: stick in place on the unprinted side: face, hair front and crown.
- ❑ For both, make up box.
- ❑ Using sticky paper, turn the box so that the back of the head is facing you. Stick on hands, coat, back of hair and crown.
- ❑ As the wise man is bringing a gift, you could put a small gift such as chocolate buttons in the box before the children take them home.

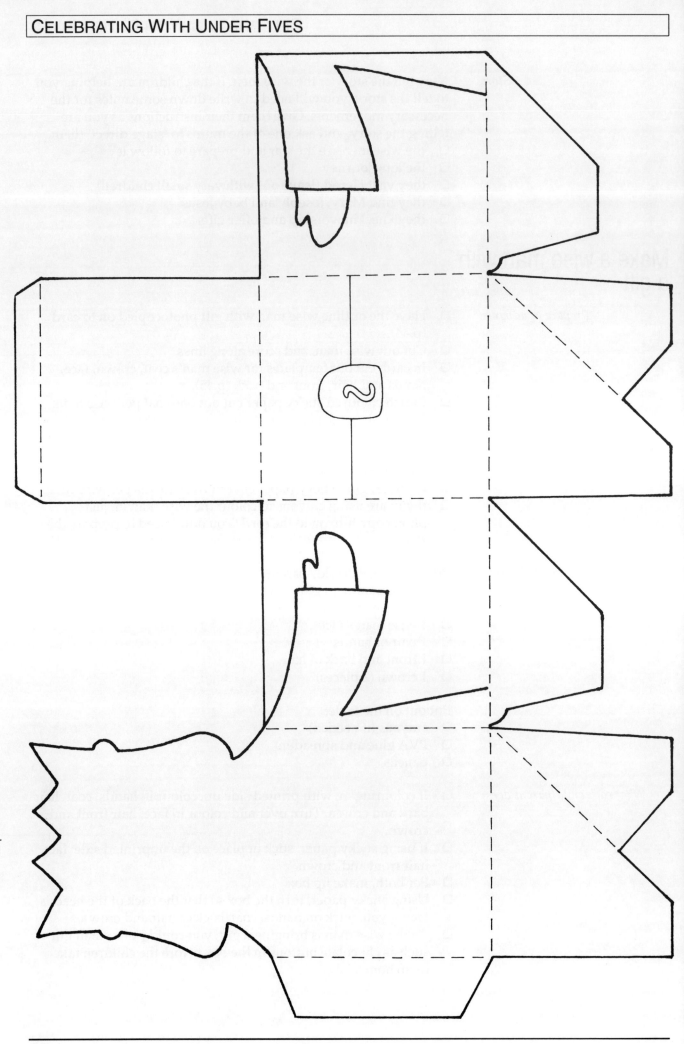

TRUE MEANING OF CHRISTMAS EVENING

Invitations

A 'True meaning of Christmas' evening is a marvellous way to revive the spirit of Christmas and introduce your neighbours to the meaning of Christmas. It has been successfully tried in a number of churches.

First make a list of special friends and relatives. Invite them and your neighbours from seven houses to your left, seven to your right and fourteen houses opposite.

If you invite strangers, you may need to send out ten times as many invitations as you expect people to come. If you invite your friends, you might well get everyone to come. Do not invite a lot of people from church, or non-churchgoers may be intimidated.

The invitation could read:

Dear Dave and Sue,

You are invited to a 'True Meaning of Christmas Evening'. Please come for about 7.30pm. We'll be singing some favourite Christmas carols and eating mince pies. Then we'll take ten minutes to hear the Christmas story and think about its true meaning, followed by a glass of wine or a cup of tea to end with.

We've invited the rest of the neighbours too. It might seem a bit old fashioned but we think it would be a good idea to get together at Christmas time. Bring the children if you want to. Please let us know whether you can come or not.

Love,

Mark and Ruth

Preparation

Preparation is very important. On the night it is important that you are organized enough to relax. You will need to:

- ❑ Send out invitations a week to ten days in advance.
- ❑ Beg or borrow enough carol sheets for everyone. If possible, get a guitarist, pianist, recorder player or good singer too.
- ❑ Be willing yourself, or invite someone else, to read the story of the birth of Jesus and to spend five minutes talking about the importance of making room for Jesus in our lives today.
- ❑ Have some sheets with details of Christmas services at your church to hand out.
- ❑ Cook mince pies and prepare drink.
- ❑ Trim up the house for the evening. Candlelight is very atmospheric.

During the evening

As people arrive, hand them something to eat and drink. Have Christmas music playing softly on a tape or record.

When enough people have come, introduce everyone and hand out carol sheets. Sing some carols. Keep the atmosphere nice and easy. Have the carols planned in advance but take requests if they are asked for. (Some people find it better to talk about the meaning of the carols as they go than to have a talk later – but don't get heavy.)

Have a reading from one of the Gospels about the birth of Jesus. Use ten Bible verses at most. Then give the short talk.

Sometimes a short ritual can help concentrate people's attention. 'I'm going to light a candle now, to remind us of Jesus Christ, the light who has come into the world. Let's be quiet for a few seconds.' Then begin the talk.

Immediately the talk finishes bring in food and/or drink. This is most important. It encourages everyone to break up into groups and chat and avoids awkward silences.

Don't forget to end the evening cheerily by wishing your guests 'Happy Christmas'. Give them a leaflet with details of Christmas services at church. Ask them if they want to come carol singing with you.

If funds will run to it, you may want to give to each guest a copy of the evangelistic booklet *What's the Point of Christmas?* by J. John. These can be ordered singly or in packs from Lion Publishing or CPAS Sales (0926 334242).

■ Reference Booklist

Further resources from CPAS

1992 CPAS code	Title	Author and publisher
02168	The Dramatised Bible	Bible Society/Marshalls
00384	The First Christmas	Lion Publishing (Children's Video Bible)
92420	Celebrating the Festivals	Sue Kirby, CPAS
	(Other books in the same series)	
92421	Stories Jesus Told	Sue Kirby, CPAS
92422	People Jesus Met	Sue Kirby, CPAS
92423	God's Special Friends	Sue Kirby, CPAS

Other evangelistic books

03471	What's the Point?	Norman Warren, Lion Publishing
03470	Ten Myths	Michael Green, Lion Publishing
03473	Resurrection – fact or fiction?	Richard Bewes, Lion Publishing
03474	A Certain Faith	Norman Warren, Lion Publishing
03472	A New Dimension	Michael Green, Lion Publishing
03498	What Happens after Death?	David Winter, Lion Publishing
03486	What's the Point of Christmas?	J. John, Lion Publishing

Hymn books

Carols for Today	Jubilate, Hodder and Stoughton
Carol Praise	Jubilate, Hodder and Stoughton
Carolling	Jubilate, Hodder and Stoughton
Play Carol Praise	Jubilate, Hodder and Stoughton

Banner-making books

An Army with Banners	Miss Priscilla Nunnerly, 9 Chestnut Court,
Banners in His name	Chestnut Lane, Amersham, Bucks, HP6 6ED
Banner Makers to the King	

■ Acknowledgements

Family Service Talks: Adapted from contributions by Andrew Body, Derek Frank, John Moore, Ripon Diocesan Board of Ministry and Training, John Short, Andrew Tremlett

Christmas Stories: J. John, Ripon Diocesan Board of Ministry and Training

Two Illustrated Talks: Pip Berry, Martin Green

Seed Ideas: Adapted from contributions by Wallace Benn, Richard Bewes, David Bird, Ian Chisholm, Andrew Dow, Keith Hallett, Peter Larkin, John Moore, Michael Moynagh, Jim Neill, Charles Riggs, Stuart Turley

Drama Sketches: No Room – Anna Jones; Special Offer – David McIntosh; Born to Die – Elizabeth Dickens; Mime for Infants – *Church Leadership Pack No 13* CPAS; Christmas Then and Now – Gill Welford

Advent Party: Eileen Moore

Celebrating with Under Fives: Sue Kirby, *Celebrating the Festivals* CPAS

Banners for Christmas: Rachel McHugh

Copyright © 1992 CPAS

Published by
Church Pastoral Aid Society
Athena Drive
Tachbrook Park
WARWICK
CV34 6NG

Telephone: (0926) 334242
Orderline: (0926) 335855
Registered Charity No 1007820
A company limited by guarantee

First edition 1992
ISBN 0 9077 50176

All rights reserved. Permission is given for purchasers to copy the illustrations on to acetates for sermons and talks provided the CPAS copyright notice is retained on each sheet.

Illustrations on pages 19 and 20 by Doug Hewitt

Editorial and design by
AD Publishing Services Ltd
Telephone: (0296) 661273

Printed by Unigraph Printing Services, Sheffield

British Library Cataloguing-in-Publication Data: A catalogue record for this book is available from the British Library